SCIENCE OF THE EARLY AMERICAN INDIANS

BEULAH AND HAROLD E. TANNENBAUM

SCIENCE OF THE EARLY AMERICAN INDIANS

FRANKLIN PIERCE
COLLEGE LIBRARY
RINDGE, N.H. 03461

Franklin Watts   1988
New York   London   Toronto   Sydney
A First Book

Cover photograph by John Curtis, Taurus Photos, Inc.

Photographs courtesy of: Robert and Linda Mitchell, Natural History
Photography: pp. 11 (Robert Mitchell), 37; Bruce Coleman, Inc.: pp. 17 (top-
John Elk III), 17 (bottom-Neyia Freeman); National Park Service Photo:
p. 22 (Richard Frear); From Charles Singer, A History of Technology,
Oxford University Press: p. 25 (both); Henry Rasof: pp. 28 (both); 81;
National Library of Medicine: p. 31; National Archives: p. 32; Sachsische
Landesbibliothek, Dresden. Used by permission.: p. 38; Jack Richard
Photo Studio, Cody, Wyoming: p. 40; Sheridan Photo Library: pp. 44 (Richard
Stirling), 85 (John P. Stevens); Field Museum of Natural History, Chicago:
p. 51; New York Public Library Picture Collection: p. 58; Library of
Congress: p. 60; Smithsonian Institute: pp. 67 (Bureau of American
Ethnology Collection), 76 (Chip Clark, The National Museum of Natural
History); Coldwater Creek, Sandpoint, Idaho: p. 83; Marilyn Bridges: p. 87.

Illustrations by Vantage Art, Inc.

Library of Congress Cataloging–in–Publication Data

Tannenbaum, Beulah.
Science of the early American Indians.

(A First book)
Bibliography: p.
Includes index.
Summary: Discusses the scientific, architectural,
astronomical, agricultural, and artistic innovations
of American Indians before the arrival of Columbus.
1. Indians—Juvenile literature. [1. Indians.
2. Science—America—History. 3. Technology—America—
History. 4. Science, Ancient] I. Tannenbaum, Harold E.
II. Title.
E58.T26 1988   509.7   87–25313
ISBN 0-531-10488-5

Copyright © 1988 by Beulah Tannenbaum and Harold E. Tannenbaum
All rights reserved
Printed in the United States of America
6 5 4 3

CURR
E
58
.T26
.1988

CONTENTS

SCIENCE OF
THE EARLY AMERICAN
INDIANS

1

INDIANS, INDIANS, AND MORE INDIANS

Try to imagine a world without wheels: no bicycles, no roller skates or skateboards, no school buses, no automobiles, no trucks, no subways, no trains, no airplanes—not even spinning wheels, carts, or chariots. It may seem that such a world could not exist. Yet before Columbus and other explorers reached the shores of the Americas, all the peoples there lived without the wheel. From the Eskimo and Aleuts in Alaska to the Fuegians of Tierra del Fuego off the southern tip of Argentina, no tribe had ever made a turning wheel work for them. The wheel was first used at least five thousand years ago in other parts of the world, but people in the Americas did not employ it until the Europeans came to stay.

The earliest Americans migrated from Asia across a land bridge more than twenty thousand years ago. They came from Siberia and crossed back and forth to North America for centuries in search of food; they were hunters and followed the roaming herds of animals. They wandered all over North America and down through Central America, or Mesoamerica, to the very tip of South America. Eventually, at the end of the last Ice Age, when the glaciers melted and the level of the oceans rose, the land bridge that they had used was flooded. So they remained in the Americas and lost contact with the rest of the world.

When Columbus arrived in 1492, he believed he had reached Asia. He was looking for a westward sea route to China to trade for silks and spices; he thought he had landed in India by mistake. So he called the natives who met him Indians, although they are not related to the Indians who live in Asia. Today we can call the Indians who lived (and still live) in North America, Mesoamerica, and South America American Indians—or Amerinds for short. North American Indians are also called Native Americans.

Early Amerinds did not have the wheel; but that does not mean they lived like cave dwellers. Their cultures varied from tribe to tribe; after all, Amerinds inhabited almost half the world. Some tribes excelled in astronomy. Some were master builders. Others were expert craftspeople. All fed, clothed, and provided shelter for themselves.

Amerinds were very religious; almost everything they did was linked to their beliefs in gods and natural spirits. It is impossible to separate their scientific achievements from their philosophical and religious beliefs. The roles of the astronomer and the priest were the same; one man was an astronomer-priest. This interrelationship is not much different from what happened elsewhere in the world. For example, as late as the nineteenth century in Europe, science was called "natural philosophy."

Our story is about the achievements of Amerinds in the period known as pre-Columbian, or the time before Columbus. Although Columbus and his crew members did little to change the way the Amerinds lived, the European conquerors, missionaries, and settlers who followed him put an end to the pre-Columbian era. In Mesoamerica we date the change at 1521, when Hernando Cortés ravaged Montezuma's Aztec empire in Mexico. In South America the date is 1530, when Francisco Pizarro shattered Atahulapa's

A nineteenth-century Navajo wall painting
of a procession of Spaniards

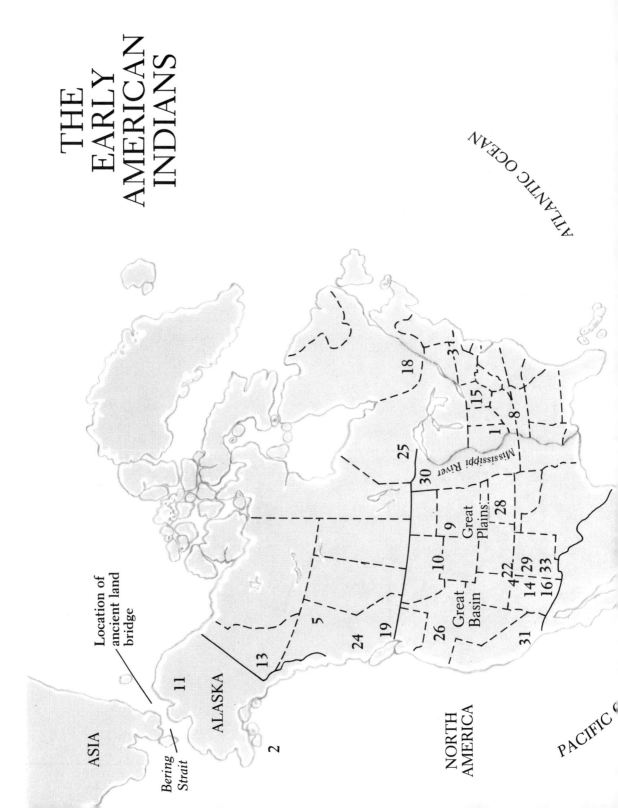

THE
EARLY
AMERICAN INDIANS

ASIA

Bering
Strait

Location of
ancient land
bridge

11

ALASKA

2

13

5

24

19

26

Great
Basin

31

4

22

29

14

16

33

Great
Plains

28

9

10

30

25

Mississippi River

18

1

15

8

3

NORTH
AMERICA

PACIFIC O

ATLANTIC OCEAN

SOUTH
AMERICA

ATLANTIC OCEAN

MESOAMERICA

Tierra Del Fuego

17   23   6   27   12

Tribe	Location
1. ADENA	Mississippi Valley
2. ALEUT	Alaska (Aleutian Islands)
3. ALGONQUIN	Northeastern United States
4. ANASAZI	Arizona, Colorado
5. ATHABASCAN	Northwestern Canada (Yukon)
6. AYMARA	Bolivia
7. AZTEC	Mexico
8. CHEROKEE	Kentucky, Tennessee
9. CHEYENNE	Great Plains
10. CROW	Wyoming, Montana
11. ESKIMO	Alaska
12. FUEGIAN	Tierra Del Fuego
13. HAIDA	Northern Pacific coast of Canada
14. HOHOKAM	Arizona
15. HOPEWELL	Ohio
16. HOPI	Arizona
17. INCA	Peru (Andes)
18. IROQUOIS	Eastern U.S. and Canada
19. KWAKIUTL	Pacific coast of Canada (Vancouver)
20. MAYA	Mexico (Yucatan), Guatemala, El Salvador
21. MIXTEC	Southwest coast of Mexico
22. NAVAJO	Arizona, Colorado
23. NAZCA	Peru (southern coast)
24. NOOTKA	Northwestern coast of Canada
25. OJIBWA	Lake Superior
26. PAIUTE	Great Basin
27. PATAGONIAN	Argentina
28. PAWNEE	Great Plains
29. PUEBLO	Arizona, New Mexico
30. SIOUX	Minnesota
31. YOKUT	California (southern coast)
32. ZAPOTEC	Southwestern Mexico
33. ZUNI	New Mexico

Inca empire in Peru. And in southwestern North America it is 1540, when Francisco de Coronado ended his vain search for the seven golden cities of Cibola by destroying the Zuni villages in New Mexico.

We know about pre-Columbian civilizations because archaeologists who have gone on digs all over the Americas have found evidence of their accomplishments. They have dated their findings by various methods, mainly by measuring the amount of radioactivity in the carbon 14 (radiocarbon) found at the sites.

We cannot detail the science and technology of each of the hundreds of tribes that lived in the Americas. But we will describe some of the achievements of the Amerind tribes and societies listed on the map.

2

FROM SUNUP TO SUNDOWN ALL THE YEAR ROUND

Science means "knowledge" or "knowing." Amerinds made use of science in the sense that they had the knowledge and skills needed to adapt their lives to their environment. They built all kinds of structures from earthen mounds to cities on cliffs. They developed many ways of making fire for cooking and heating. They utilized a variety of crops. And they practiced medicine in different forms.

Amerinds lived in communities—some large, some consisting of only a few families. The Paiute villages in North America rarely had more than 100 people. But other tribes, like the Adena Mound Builders of Cahokia, on the eastern bank of the Mississippi River across from where the city of St. Louis now is, lived in earthen houses in urban complexes that may have had as many as 30,000 people. Some communities were even larger. The Spaniards who accompanied Cortés came upon Tenochtitlán (teh NOK teh TLAN) in Mexico, where Montezuma ruled the Aztecs. Before Cortés destroyed it, this was a city of more than 250,000 people, about as many as live in present-day Akron, Ohio, or twice as many as live in Trenton, New Jersey.

EARTHEN MOUNDS

Perhaps the most visible signs of Amerinds' technological ability are the burial, temple, and dwelling mounds of the Adena. More than 100,000 of these mounds exist in the United States. They can be found throughout the valleys of the Mississippi and its tributaries, as is obvious from such place names as Moundville, Alabama; Moundville, Missouri; Moundsville, Ohio; Moundsville, West Virginia; Mound City, Illinois; Mound City, Missouri; Mound City, Kansas; Mound City, South Dakota; Mound Bayou, Mississippi; and Mound Valley, Kansas.

As a group, these mounds are a greater achievement than the Egyptian pyramids. For example, compare the Cahokia mound with the pyramid of the Pharoah Cheops at Gizeh. The Cahokia mound is not as high as the pyramid, but its base is 750,000 square feet (70,000 sq m) larger. It is estimated that to build the mound at Poverty Point, Louisiana, 660,000 cubic yards (500,000 cu m) of earth had to be moved; 3 million man-hours of labor were involved. That is the same amount of earth as could be carried by forty freight trains, each more than 1 mile (1.6 km) long and pulling one hundred large ore cars filled with earth, and as much labor as could be performed by a thousand people, each working three thousand hours or three hundred ten-hour days. And they moved all the earth without wheelbarrows.

Above: an earthen mound in Winterville, Mississippi. Below: a modern Navajo earth house, or hogan, in Monument Valley, Arizona.

16

HOUSES

Regardless of where they lived or the size of their communities, Amerinds used the building materials available to them for housing and adapted their houses to their surroundings. Some of their housing was temporary, like the summer huts of the Paiute, who roamed over the Great Basin hunting and gathering seeds. But building even these huts required skill. The Paiute knew how to form a perfect circle, and so they erected tent-shaped, circular structures of saplings. They drove saplings into the ground close together in a circle and bound the tops in a point. Paiute may have had only a natural understanding of geometry, but their results were practical.

Like the Adena, the Pawnee, who lived on the Great Plains, built earthen houses. For each house they erected four support posts and placed rafters across them. Then they tamped earth around this frame and over the top to form a domed roof. There were no windows and only one entrance, which always faced east.

The orientation of their houses was the most important factor in their construction because the Pawnee needed to be able to make astronomical observations. Their entire lives were closely coordinated with the movements of the heavenly bodies. So the four posts were not placed at random. One post was midway between north and east; the next was midway between east and south; the third was between south and west; and the fourth was between west and north. Imaginary lines from these posts to the eastern and western horizons marked off the northern and southern boundaries of the sky between which the sun, the moon, and the morning and evening stars could always be found.

In Tenochtitlán—present-day Mexico City—there were thousands of buildings—temples, palaces, and houses for the common people. Most Aztecs lived in windowless, one-room earthen huts

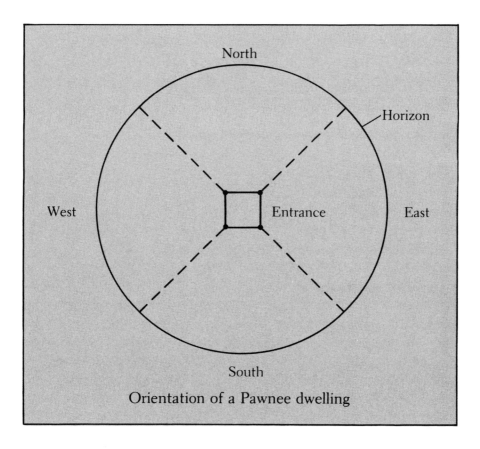

North

Horizon

West

Entrance

East

South

Orientation of a Pawnee dwelling

similar to those of the Pawnee: they had reed and mud walls and roofs of reed and grass. The temples and palaces for the nobles had many rooms and were built to last. Some were made of stone, cut into blocks and piled several stories high. We know that the builders understood structural stress because the stone walls taper inward slightly, reducing the strain on the upper levels.

Most of the buildings were of **adobe**—one of the great contributions of the Amerinds. Adobe is sun-dried brick made from mud or clay and mixed with straw for strength. An oblong wooden mold without a bottom is filled with clay-straw mixture, shaping a brick. The mold is lifted off, and the brick is left on the ground to dry and harden in the sun. Adobe was—and still is—used throughout Mesoamerica and the Southwest. It is ideal for the climate, since it is a good insulator; it keeps buildings relatively cool in summer and warm in winter, especially if the windows and entrances are few and small.

The Haida of the Northwest, on the coast of British Columbia, lived in large log houses at the edges of forests of tall trees. Because the trees they cut for logs were so tall, the long logs could be placed lengthwise to form *long houses*. Each village had thirty or more long houses lined up with their doors facing the beach. A number of related families lived in each house; the family totem pole was erected alongside.

Farther north, in Alaska, there were no big trees or even saplings for houses. Because of the permafrost the Eskimo could not dig up the earth, either. But they were clever enough to use what they had: blocks of frozen snow. The Eskimo built dome-shaped igloos by piling the snow blocks upward in a spiral. These provided adequate shelter in the bitter winter but were useless during prolonged thaws.

CLIFF DWELLINGS
AND PUEBLOS

In sections of Arizona and Colorado huge outcroppings of rock form high cliffs. Strange structures jut out from the cliff walls, the "apartment houses" of the cliff dwellers. The cliff dwellers built their homes right into the cliff walls, making use of the natural caves there and supplementing them with adobe structures. The most famous of the "apartment houses" still in existence are Montezuma Castle in Central Arizona and Mesa Verde in southwestern Colorado. Montezuma Castle was named by pioneers, but it has no connection with Montezuma, the Emperor of the Aztecs. Montezuma Castle was built by the Anasazi eight hundred years ago, at least three hundred years before Montezuma lived. At Mesa Verde, which is about 2,300 feet (700 m) above the surrounding countryside, there are some three hundred dwellings and twenty-three meeting rooms, called **kivas,** which were inhabited almost until the year 1300.

The construction of these lofty cliff dwellings required considerable skill. The builders had to make the best use of available openings in the rock and add on to them while at the same time not making them too accessible from below. The cliff's advantage was that it gave the cliff dwellers excellent protection from enemies, especially from the Navajo, who were invading that area at that time. But its drawback was that the vegetable gardens that the cliff dwellers tended had to be at a distance—on level land. They had to carry all the water they needed up the steep cliff, as well.

These communal dwellings were called **pueblos** by the Spaniards; *pueblo* is the Spanish word for "people." Although the Zuni pueblos were not in cliffs, they also had no ground-level entrances. Ladders were placed against the sides of their adobe buildings; the Zunis climbed to the roofs and then eased themselves down through openings into the rooms below. The ladders were pulled up and stored on the roofs, leaving no access for strangers. One Zuni village, Pueblo Aztec, had four hundred rooms and a Great Kiva that was 43 feet (13 m) in diameter. The building of the Great Kiva, a large round room, required great skill. In Pueblo Bonita, 1,200 people lived in eight hundred rooms. These settlements were often abandoned; we are not sure why. Perhaps it was due to lack of water, or perhaps to enemy raids. But in Pecos, near Santa Fe, New Mexico, six towns were built over the years, one on

top of the other. Sometimes newer ones used parts of older structures. A few pueblos are still in use; one is Taos Pueblo, with its ladders and roof entrances.

COOKING AND FIRE MAKING

Coronado found no doors studded with gold or gems and no golden dishes in the Southwest, which may have disappointed him, but he did find thriving communities with large maize and bean fields and lots of "large chickens."

The "large chickens" that Coronado saw may well have been turkeys. Amerinds kept dogs and turkeys, but they domesticated few animals for food. Most of the flesh they ate came instead from game they hunted or from fish they caught. Game and fish were roasted over open fires or stewed in water in baskets or clay pots.

Today when we heat water, we put a pot over a fire or other source of heat. But Amerinds did it differently; they heated stones in a fire and then put the hot stones into the water, raising it to the desired temperature. This method was satisfactory because stones retain heat well and gradually release it into water.

Open fires were also used to heat dwellings in cold weather. They also provided most of the light at night. In their igloos the Eskimo often used stone "lamps" for all three purposes—cooking, heating, and light. Their "lamps" were hollowed-out stones in which the blubber of walruses or seals was burned; twisted moss was used for wicks. Whenever fuel was adequate, the fires were

Montezuma Castle,
in central Arizona

kept burning because although rekindling them was fairly easy, it was a nuisance. Amerinds couldn't just strike a match, the way we can.

To start their fires, Amerinds usually rubbed one piece of wood against another to produce friction. The heat generated by friction caused the wood dust created by such rubbing to smolder. The smoldering heap was blown into a glowing mass that set fire to tinder, which was often placed so that the dust would fall on it as it was produced.

One tool for making fire that was used by Amerinds, from the Eskimo in the north to the Aztecs in Mexico to the Aymará in Bolivia, was the fire drill. The fire drill was a two-stick apparatus. One piece of wood, the hearth, was held still on the ground. The other, a cylindrical or tapering drill, was held vertically and rotated back and forth (in reciprocating motion) while being pressed downward into the hearth. This created friction and heat.

Different tribes had different methods of operating the drill. The simplest, that of the Aymará, was to hold the drill between the palms of both hands and twirl it back and forth while pressing it into a shallow pit in the hearth. In a two- or three-person method such as the Maya used, one person worked the drill while the others held the hearth steady.

To improve the efficiency of the back-and-forth rotation and the ease of the drill's operation, a cord or thong was wound around the drill in a single loop. Each end of the thong had a wooden or bone handle that a fire maker could hold easily, one in each hand. The thong was pulled first with one hand and then with the other, so that the drill changed its direction repeatedly, rotating back and forth. But the drill also had to be held upright and pressed downward into the hearth. To do this, a socket holder of wood, bone, or stone was fitted snugly over the drill. Since both of the fire maker's hands were already employed in the reciprocating motion, an extra person was needed to press down on the socket holder. The Eski-

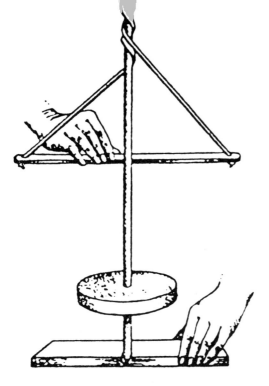

Firemaking tools
and methods

pump drill

Aymará Indian using a fire drill

mo kept the thong drill a one-person operation by devising a special socket holder. They shaped it so that it could be gripped in the mouth of the fire maker. While pulling on the thong with both hands, the fire maker could apply pressure with the jaw.

Another adaptation of the fire drill that was used by Eskimo and other North American tribes was the bow drill. The bow was a short stick or stave, often curved; a thong was loosely attached at both ends, like a bowstring. The thong was then looped around the drill. A fire maker used one hand to press down on the socket piece of the drill and used the other to rotate the drill by alternately pulling and pushing the bow.

The Iroquois used another adaptation; they invented a pump drill. The pump drill required two pieces of thong. One end of each thong was attached to the top of the drill. The other end of each was attached to a cross piece. The Iroquois achieved back-and-forth rotation by pumping up and down on the cross piece with one hand and holding the hearth steady with the other.

A means of fire making that was less common than the drills was to strike a piece of flint against a stone containing iron pyrite ("fool's gold") and let sparks fall onto kindling. The Eskimo and a few other Indians of North America and the Fuegians of South America sometimes started fires this way.

FOOD AND BEVERAGES

Cooking fires were used for vegetables more than for meat, especially among Amerinds who were farmers. Their chief crop was **maize**, which we call corn. *Corn* is an old word that originally meant "hard seed" or "kernel"; it was used in that sense in such words as *barleycorn* and *peppercorn*. Now it is generally used to refer to the major grain of an area. Wheat in England is called "corn." In Scotland rye is "corn." In the Americas maize is "corn."

Maize must be planted; it does not sow itself. We have evidence that Amerinds started growing maize more than seven thousand years ago in both Mexico and Peru. By 1500 B.C. it was the major crop in Mexico. In the southwest the Pueblo Indians grew many maize varieties: yellow, white, black, blue, pink, and even speckled. Maize was not introduced into New England until about the year 1400; but by the time the Europeans arrived, two hundred years later, the Iroquois had more than fifty recipes for serving it. These included corn on the cob, hominy, mush, popcorn, cornbread, puddings, succotash (a mixture of corn and beans), and several kinds of corn soup.

Amerinds knew that moist vegetables rot if they are left untreated, so they often dried their maize. They dried it on the cob or in whole kernels or in cracked kernels and then stored it in baskets for later use.

The most common way to preserve corn was to grind it into flour or meal. To do this they placed maize kernels onto a stone slab that had a slight hollow in it, called a **metate**; they then ground the kernels with a large pebble or stone that could be held in the hand, called a **mano**. (In these words we find the influence of the Spaniards on Amerinds. *Mano* is the Spanish word for "hand"; *metate* is a Spanish version of the Aztec word *metlatl*.)

Sometimes a metate could be a hollow in an outcropping of bedrock. There are many such metates at the top of Tumacoc Hill, within the city limits of Tucson, Arizona. About a thousand years ago, this hill was a sacred place. There, at harvest time, the Hohokam brought their maize to thank the spirits for the crop. By climbing up several hundred yards (meters) from their dwellings along the Santa Cruz River, they felt that they were coming closer to the spirits that provided the maize; they honored them by grinding it into meal in their presence.

Cornmeal could be kept for a long time. One way some Amerinds used it was to bake it on a flat stone over an open fire, making

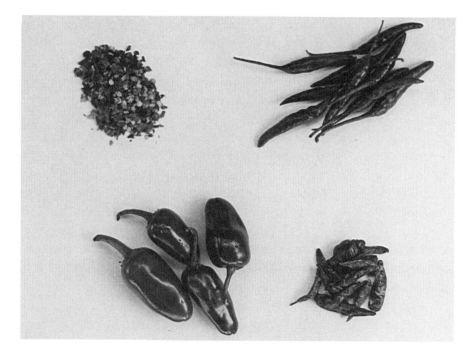

Above: chile peppers and seeds. The big
peppers are jalapeños. Below: metates used to
grind acorns. These are in Cuyamaca Rancho
State Park, near Julian, California.

tortillas. In some parts of the Southwest and in Mesoamerica it is still done that way.

Amerinds also grew and dried pinto beans, lima beans, pink beans, peanuts, and chili peppers. They cut summer squash, acorn squash, and pumpkins into strips and dried them in the sun. They saved pumpkin seeds and shelled them to nibble on later.

What we call white or Irish potatoes actually originated in the New World. The Spaniards introduced them into Europe, where they became the staple crop of many countries, especially Ireland. The Incas grew several varieties of potatoes: white, pinkish-gray, purple, black, spotted, and streaked. They also had a special way to preserve them. First they placed the potatoes out in the cold mountain air, where they alternately froze and thawed. Then, on and off for four or five days, they trampled on them with their bare feet to squeeze out the moisture. This resulted in fully dehydrated potatoes that could be either stored whole or ground with a mano and metate into potato flour, which today is called chuño (CHOO nyo).

Another cereal crop that grew well high up in the Andes was quinoa. The Inca used quinoa plants' small white, red, or black seeds in soup. When boiled, quinoa seeds split open and send out white threads that look like fine noodles. (Quinoa is available in some health-food stores and in stores that carry Mexican or South American products.)

To drink, the Maya and the Aztecs were particularly fond of cocoa. They got cocoa beans from **cacao** trees. These trees grow only in the area between ten degrees north of the equator and ten degrees south of the equator—from Costa Rica to Brazil—and between 100 and 1,000 feet (30 and 300 m) above sea level. Each cacao tree bears about thirty large pods that are shaped like footballs but are only half the size. Each pod contains between twenty and forty seeds, or beans. The Aztecs ground cacao beans in metates that were hollowed out of lava, a volcanic rock. They added crushed chili peppers and brewed the mixture into a very pungent drink. The Spaniards did not like cocoa that sharp, so they substituted sugar for the peppers, as we do today.

Amerinds also grew tomatoes, avocados, sweet potatoes, amaranth, manioc (cassava), and gourds. They ate wild seeds and berries that they collected; sometimes they prepared them specially. For example, the Anasazi boiled the fruit of the prickly-pear cactus to make jelly.

MEDICINE

There are more ways than one to cure an illness. The Chinese introduced acupuncture, inserting needles at pressure points on the body. Other people use drugs to make sick people well. Still others change the diet—what a patient eats—to effect a cure. And still others—chiropractors—manipulate the bones of the body to restore health. Finally, psychiatrists, who believe that certain illnesses are caused by a patient's mental state, treat the mind to cure the body.

Amerinds used—and still use—most of these means to heal a sick person. They believed in addition that evil spirits could harm a body; so besides treating the body, they also used songs and spells to drive off the evil spirits. However, their knowledge of the therapeutic value of certain herbs, barks, and roots cured most ailments.

Most Amerind healers were men. The dictionary defines *medicine man* as "a priestly healer." Medicine men were both seers—links to the spiritual world—and healers. As healers, they

*Inside a North American
Indian medicine lodge*

30

A twentieth-century medicine lodge

employed various techniques. They massaged an affected area; they cut into blood vessels and bled a patient to remove an infection. They repaired broken bones, as the Sioux did, by wrapping a set bone in a piece of rawhide (untanned animal skin). They soaked the rawhide till it was very soft and tied it in place with rawhide bands. As the rawhide dried and shrank, it molded itself to the arm or leg, forming a cast similar to the plaster casts used in the United States today.

Medicine men made inhalers by placing certain herbs or roots on hot coals and having a patient breathe in the fumes. A small tent was made from a blanket or cloth and placed around the fire and over the patient's head; this increased the concentration of the fumes. They cured patients' fever by putting them in sweat lodges—enclosed structures in which open fires kept the air temperature very high. Or they treated patients directly with infusions or teas of various herbs or by placing pasty mixtures of herbs on affected areas.

An experienced medicine man had a store of several hundred plants, herbs, and barks; he knew at what stage of growth each was at its best for medicinal use. Some were boiled and given to a patient as a brew or tea to drink. Some were chewed or pounded into a powder to make a paste that could be applied to the wound. Sometimes a patient was given a root to chew on, such as wild licorice to ease a toothache. Sometimes medicine men dried the leaves of plants and gave them to patients to smoke in a pipe—for example, dried jimsonweed to treat asthma, cholera, or epilepsy.

Medicine men used more than twenty-five different plants to combat snakebites, one of the most common ailments. There were also several remedies for nosebleeds, stomachaches, and bowel problems. They used the juice from the stems and leaves of jewelweed to cure poison ivy. Centuries before aspirin was invented, they treated headaches and fevers with willow bark. Willow bark contains an ingredient now used to make aspirin. They boiled the leaves of horsemint to cure acne. They steeped the root of valerian to make a mild sedative against nervous disorders, hysteria, and delirium.

Today we realize that many of the medicine men's remedies were sound procedures, even though they may have been intermingled with spells and charms to invoke spirits. For too long our educational background has conditioned us to believe that "modern" and "scientific" are good and that "traditional" or "spiritual" are bad.

WHAT THE GODS ORDAIN

When archaeologists first speculated about the purpose of the ruined structures of Amerinds, a few thought that they had definite astronomical meaning because of their alignments with the stars and other heavenly bodies. But others said these alignments were accidental. They did not believe that Amerinds were capable of scientific activity because their methods did not fit the modern concept of science. Modern scientists have tried to understand humans' relationship with the natural world so that they could control their environment. But Amerinds believed that spirits controlled the universe, not humans; they tried instead to predict the negative forces in the world so that they could avoid calamities.

OBSERVING THE SKY

Like ancient peoples all over the world, Amerinds believed that each heavenly body was related to a god or spirit. The most important were the sun, the moon, and the planet Venus; some tribes also kept track of such stars as the Pleiades and Sirius. From watching the heavens year after year, Amerinds recognized that certain events recurred regularly; so they created calendars to keep track of them. This was important to do so that they would know when to prepare the land for planting, when the rainy season would start, when they needed to harvest their crops before the first frost, and when they had to leave their summer hunting campgrounds before the snows came.

The North American Indians had no system of writing, so they left no written records of their astronomical observations. However, we can reconstruct some of their knowledge from their structures that remain and from their **petroglyphs**—or rock pictures. In Mesoamerica the Maya and the Aztecs had a hieroglyphic system of writing. They used rebuses, or pictures, to represent words and syllables; they also used different colors, each of which had a special meaning.

Scientists have yet to decipher completely their written language. But they continue to study the Aztec and Mayan codices (singular: **codex**), painted books made from strips of deerskin or pressed tree bark, sewn together in long panels, and folded like a screen. In these codices the Aztecs and the Maya recorded their astronomical and mathematical knowledge as well as instructions for agriculture and craftwork. The Spaniards, in their zeal to convert Amerinds to Christianity and root out anything they considered pagan, burned all the codices they could find. Only four escaped the flames. They are now in museums in Europe.

To prepare astronomical tables for their codices and to predict changes in the seasons, the Aztecs and Maya recorded what they observed in the sky. It was obvious to them that the sun rises in the east and sets in the west. (We now know that the sun does not move across the sky; the earth rotates daily on its axis from west to east as it travels completely around the sun each year.) It was also obvious that sunrise and sunset do not occur at the same spots on the horizon every day. In the Northern Hemisphere in summer the sun rises and sets farther north than it does in winter. This shift

Petroglyphs on Newspaper Rock, in Utah

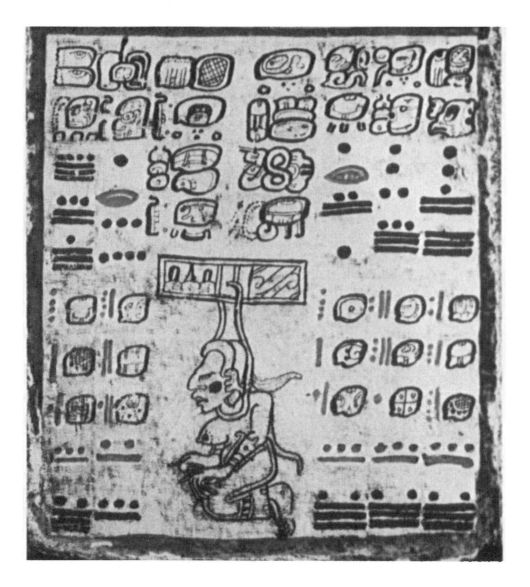

Mayan lunar tables from a book kept
in Germany called the Dresden Codex

is due to the tilt of the earth's axis in relation to the sun. In summer the Northern Hemisphere is tilted toward the sun; in winter it is tilted away from the sun.

The day of the most northerly sunrise is the summer **solstice**, which falls on or about June 21. On that day in the Northern Hemisphere, summer begins. It is also the longest day of the year—it has the greatest number of hours between sunrise and sunset. In the Southern Hemisphere on June 21, it is just the opposite. The southern part of the earth is tilted away from the sun, and it is the shortest day, or the beginning of winter. The most southerly sunrise occurs on the winter solstice (December 21), the beginning of winter in the north and summer in the south. The days on which the sun rises midway between these two extremes are the spring **equinox** (March 21) and the fall equinox (September 21). These four days were considered the most important days in their year; Amerinds had many ways of determining just when they occurred.

MARKING THE SOLSTICES
AND EQUINOXES

Some of the simplest devices used to observe the skies were Medicine Wheels, which were found in the western part of North America from Arizona to Alberta and Saskatchewan. To the pioneers who first saw them, they looked like huge wagon wheels. The early settlers believed that they were used for magical purposes, so they called them Medicine Wheels.

Medicine wheels were large circles of stone; they had spokes of stone radiating from the center. Some of them had piles of stone, called **cairns**, at the center. About fifty still remain; the best known is the Big Horn Medicine Wheel in Wyoming. The Crow built it at their summer campground in the Big Horn Mountains, at an

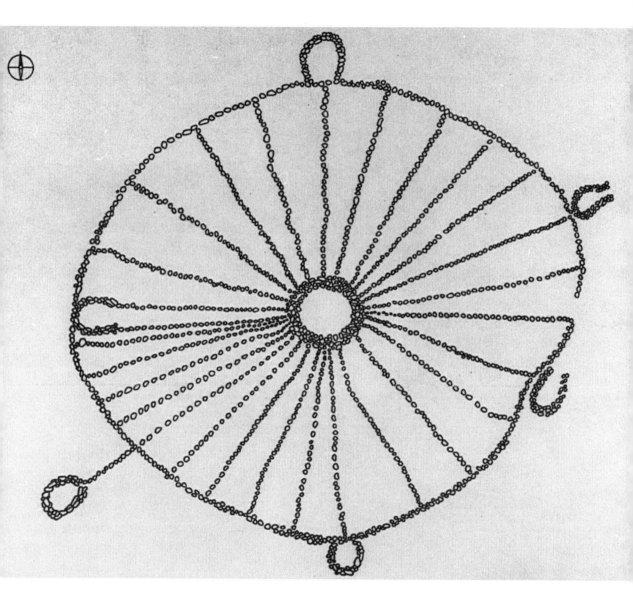

A medicine wheel

elevation of 10,500 feet (3,200 m). It is between 92 and 98 feet (28 and 30 m) across—about the size of the infield of a baseball diamond—and in the center is a cairn 12 feet (4 m) in diameter and 2 feet (60 cm) high. It has twenty-eight spokes and six U-shaped cairns around the rim: five outside the circle and one inside.

The Crow could use the Medicine Wheel to determine the summer solstice. They stood at the inside cairn and sighted the horizon along an imaginary line across the central cairn. When the sun rose at the point on the horizon at the end of this imaginary line, they knew the day had arrived. They could also observe the rising of several stars by using the various cairns along the rim. However, there was no way to observe the winter solstice; the tribe left their very high mountaintop camp before the snows came.

A more advanced method of astronomical observation made use of permanent structures. We have already seen that the Pawnee built their houses so that the four main posts were aligned with the summer and winter solstice sunrise and sunset points on the horizon. Standing alongside the northeasterly post, they looked along an imaginary line between it and another post or stone especially erected a little way off and sighted the horizon. When the sun rose over the horizon at the point at the end of this imaginary line, the Pawnee knew it was the most northerly sunrise—the summer solstice. The advantage of the two westerly posts was that if the Pawnee missed a solstice sunrise because of clouds, they could still sight the solstice sunset.

The Hohokam also used this method to determine the solstices and equinoxes. In about the year 1300 they built Casa Grande (Big House) in the desert between present-day Phoenix and Tucson. This three-story adobe structure was probably both the home of the tribal leaders and a ceremonial center or temple. From window slots punched in the walls of the upper stories, the Hohokam could get a clear view of the surrounding Great Basin, monitor their system of irrigation canals, and keep a lookout for enemies. And they could also sight the horizon.

Archaeoastronomers (scientists who study the astronomy of ancient people) have investigated the ruins of Casa Grande and have found that eight of the fourteen window slots in the upper walls are aligned with the risings and settings of the sun at the solstices and equinoxes. For example, the Hohokam knew the summer solstice had arrived when they sighted the sun rising on the horizon at the end of an imaginary line formed by the inside edge of one opening and the outside edge of another. This method, called an "alternate doorjamb" sighting was used widely throughout the pre-Columbian Americas.

A variation on this method of sighting the sunrise was the use of landmarks. A landmark could be a natural feature, such as a gap or a cleft in a high butte, as at the Wijii ruins in New Mexico. Standing at a painted sun symbol on a stone stairway 1,600 feet (500 m) away, the Pueblo Indians could observe the winter solstice sunrise framed in the gap. The landmark could also be a stone column such as Amerinds erected at Copán in Honduras. And sometimes the landmarks were entire temple complexes.

For example, at the Uaxactún, Mexico, temple complex, the Maya built temples so that each structure was a landmark. If they stood on top of a pyramid and faced east, they could watch the sun rise over three different temples across an open plaza. On the summer solstice the sun rose over the northernmost temple; on the winter solstice it rose over the southernmost temple; and on the equinoxes it rose over the central temple. The Aztecs built another temple complex at Tenochtitlán, present-day Mexico City. There the Templo Mayor (*mayor* means "principal" in Spanish) is a huge pyramid topped by two temples; across the plaza there is a cylindrical tower, the Temple of Quetzalcoatl (ket sel koh AH tel).

From the top of the tower, at the equinoxes, the Aztecs could watch the sun rise between the two opposite temples.

Other Amerinds did not have to look along imaginary lines to sight sunrises. Sometime between the years 950 and 1150 the Anasazi built a circular kiva that the Spaniards named Casa Rinconada ("Corner House") at their pueblo in Chaco Canyon, New Mexico. On the summer solstice the rising sun shines through a northeast window and lights up a niche in the opposite wall. The Cheyenne, too, built summer medicine lodges on the Great Plains so that on the summer solstice the rising sun was framed in the doorways, heralding the beginning of the summer ceremonies.

Another method that Amerinds used to mark the solstices and equinoxes was shadow casting. When the Maya built the huge pyramid of Kukulkán in Chichén Itzá, Mexico, in the ninth century, they aligned it so that an impressive shadow was formed at sunset on the equinoxes. On those days, the setting sun casts a shadow along the railing of a stairway that leads from the temple structure at the top of the pyramid to a sacred pool at the base. The shadow of the temple resembles a snake, and as the sun moves lower and lower toward the horizon, the snake seems to slither down the railing. Very dramatically, just at the moment of sunset, when the sun drops below the horizon, the snake shadow disappears into the water of the pool.

EL CARACOL

Also at Chichén Itzá is a round structure called El Caracol. It was so named by the Spaniards because its spiral staircase, which leads to the tower, reminded them of a snail or *caracol* in Spanish. The Maya designed El Caracol as a multipurpose observatory from which at least twenty events could be seen and recorded. The top of the tower of El Caracol has been destroyed, so we do not know

The Temple of Kukulkán
at Chichén Itzá, Mexico

what other observations and measurements were possible; but we do know that the Maya could observe the sunrises and sunsets at the solstices and the equinoxes from El Caracol. A picture of El Caracol is on the cover of this book.

The Maya could also make the more difficult observations of the zenith crossings of the sun—the two times each year when the sun is directly overhead at noon and no shadows are cast. The Maya believed that the shadows disappeared because the "Diving God" descended into the ground and brought on the rainy season. (Actually, the rainy season is caused by the intense heat of the vertical rays of the sun.) After the descent of the god the Maya could plant their maize and other crops confidently; the rains would surely water them.

Also from El Caracol the Maya could keep track of Venus, which was important to them for both religious and time-keeping purposes. They associated Venus with the god Kukulkán-Quetzalcoatl, who they believed had disappeared into the west with the promise to return someday out of the eastern sea. The Maya did not know that Venus was a planet revolving around the sun; from El Caracol they observed it disappearing in the west and reappearing as the morning star in the east—like the god—before the rising sun eight days later.

The Maya watched Venus closely and charted their observations. They found that sometimes Venus rose just before the sun and appeared as just a flash of light before being dimmed by the brilliant sunrise. This is called the **heliacal rising** (*helios* is the Greek word for "sun"); the Maya knew that this occurred every 584 days—a "Venus year."

The Maya figured out tables that compared the "Venus year" with the "Earth year"—365 days. They found that eight "Earth years" ($8 \times 365 = 2,920$) are the equivalent of five "Venus years" ($5 \times 584 = 2,920$); they found that after 2,920 days Venus returns to the same place in the sky at the same time of the year. They built El Caracol with several sight lines so that the most northern and most southern risings of Venus could be observed.

OBSERVATIONS OF
THE STARS AND MOON

The Maya also used El Caracol to observe the rising and setting of the group of seven stars that we know as the Pleiades or the Seven Sisters. They called them Tzab ("the rattle"—of the rattlesnake). Archaeoastronomers have found that in April of the year 1000 the Pleiades would have shone into a tower window of El Caracol, announcing the arrival of the sun at its zenith.

Other Amerinds were also concerned with observing the Pleiades. The Aztecs called them Tianquiztl ("the Marketplace") and used them to determine their most important feast day, the Binding of the Years. This feast day took place every fifty-two years, when the Pleiades crossed the zenith at midnight. The Navajo also watched the Pleiades carefully because they associated that constellation with their principal god—Black God, the creator of fire and light.

Amerinds observed other stars, too. For example, three of the cairns at the Big Horn Medicine Wheel are aligned with the helical risings of Sirius ("the Dog Star"), Aldeberan (the bright star that is the "eye" in the constellation Taurus), and Rigel (the bright star in the left foot of the constellation Orion). These stars were so important to Amerinds that even the kings were required to observe them. We know from one of the codices that the mighty Montezuma, Emperor of the Aztecs, rose at about 3 A.M. to offer incense to certain principal stars immediately before dawn. And Metzahualpilli, King of Texcoco, went up to the terraced roof of his palace each night to commune with the stars.

But the most obvious and most observed feature of the night sky that Amerinds tracked is the moon. North American tribes used the moon to measure distance as well as time. They would describe a distant place as being "three moons away," meaning that traveling on foot, it would take three lunar (moon) months to get there. They measured time from one appearance of the crescent of the new moon to the next. The Hopi combined the moon watch with the sun watch and started their year with the first appearance of the thin crescent at sunset following the summer solstice. In one of the codices is a lunar-phase table in which the Aztecs figured the length of the lunar month to be 29.52592 days, which is within seven minutes of the best modern measurement.

Amerinds were also much concerned about predicting eclipses, when the shadow of one heavenly body is cast onto another. They believed that during an eclipse the god that was related to the darkened heavenly body disappeared. The Maya, with their careful record keeping, predicted lunar eclipses as occurring on one of two dates: either 177 or 148 days after the last eclipse. Archaeoastronomers consider this a remarkable feat, especially since it was accomplished during the period of European history known as the Dark Ages. They think of it as a triumph equal to those of Newton and Einstein.

Some events in the sky do not recur, but because they are spectacular, Amerinds recorded them. Such an event took place on July 4, 1054, when an old star exploded and formed what we now call the Crab Nebula.

The Crab Nebula is a vast, expanding cloud of stellar dust with a pulsar—the collapsed core of the old star—at its center. The explosion was so violent and so bright that it could be seen in daylight for twenty-three days. We know about it because it was described by the Chinese and Japanese astronomers who saw it. But it was also observed and recorded by the Amerinds of the

Southwest. The Anasazi observed the Crab Nebula supernova—bright new star—below the crescent moon just before dawn on the northeastern horizon; they recorded it on a cave wall and on the wall of a canyon in Arizona.

Other such recordings have been found in California and New Mexico. In each location the northeastern horizon can be seen clearly; each location was inhabited in 1054. All the records show a solid circle—the new star—and a crescent moon. Some were **pictographs**—paintings on a variety of materials; some were petroglyphs—carvings in stone. We feel certain that by these means the Anasazi and Pueblo Indians communicated this strange event.

INDIAN TO INDIAN

All societies, both ancient and modern, depend on communication to live with one another, to trade with one another, and to pass on their cultures from generation to generation. Amerinds did not have an alphabet; they could not write the words of their languages. But they had many other means of communicating with each other. They also developed advanced ways of using numbers and created intricate calendars to regulate their lives.

North American Indians drew pictures on cloth, hide, or stone since they had no written language. But using pictures they could only record visual events such as the great Crab Nebula explosion of 1054 or a particularly successful hunting expedition showing the number of deer taken or a battle showing the number of enemies killed.

North American Indians could, however, leave messages for each other on trails using stones or twigs. They piled the stones like a cairn or placed them side by side. They would break or bend twigs or fork them or tie them together. These signs could indicate the direction to follow, where to make camp, or where water could

be found. They could also show whether any game was in the area and whether unfriendly tribes were nearby.

Mesoamerican Indians used **hieroglyphs,** or pictures for syllables or whole words. For example, the town of Nocheztlán in southern Mexico was named after the cochineal insect (*nochezti*), which the inhabitants used for making the red dye **cochineal.** The Aztec hieroglyph for *Nocheztlán* was a drawing of a pot containing cochineal insects and the nopal cactus on which they live. The Aztecs drew the hieroglyphs on paper, then bound them into books like the codices.

PAPER

Paper making was a very old art in Mesoamerica. A stone paper beater from three thousand years ago was found recently in Guatemala. Amerinds usually made paper by beating the inner bark of the fig or mulberry tree or leaves from the **maguey** plant into pulp, then spreading it out to dry and pressing it into sheets. The demand for paper was so great that millions of sheets were sent to the capital each year from the towns the Aztecs had conquered as tribute. Some of these towns still exist; their names include the Aztec word *amatl*, which means "paper"—for example, Amayuca—"place where paper is made"—and Amatitlán—"place of much paper."

The Aztecs used paper for many purposes besides books. They used it to represent various spirits, especially those related to agriculture. They performed religious ceremonies with paper figures to insure good rainfall and plentiful crops. They used paper for statue

Hieroglyphs for
Mayan numbers

50

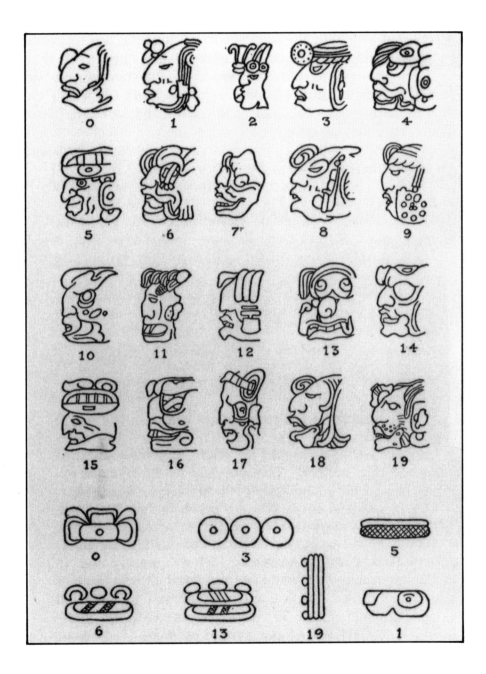

decorations, for clothes for priests representing gods, and for sacred banners and flags. At funerals slips of paper accompanied the dead on their journeys to the underworld. Everywhere paper was burned in great quantities as offerings to the spirits. Not only did the Spaniards destroy the codices to convert the Aztecs to Christianity, they also outlawed the making and use of paper. So the Aztec means of written communication—of recording their language for others—disappeared.

LANGUAGE

Pre-Columbian Amerinds spoke many different languages. This was because the tribes had migrated to the New World at different times and probably had come from different areas of Asia. Furthermore, once they reached the Americas, they settled in places far apart from one another and could not understand one another.

The languages spoken by Amerinds fall into what are called language groups. For instance, Indians in the Northwest spoke a language that belonged to the Athabascan language group. In the Northeast the language Indians spoke belonged to the Algonquian language group. In the far north the language group was Eskimo; in the Southwest it was Aztec. However, on the Great Plains the Sioux, Cheyenne, Blackfoot, Kiowa, Crow, Dakota, Pawnee, Nez Percé, and Osage had no common language group; they were peoples of different migrations. But since they all were nomadic, they often came in contact and needed to communicate with one another. To do this, they developed a system of hand signs similar to those used today by the deaf.

Some of their signs were like those used all over the world; it was natural to use them. For example, everyone points to oneself to mean *me* and to the other person to mean *you*. *Up* and *down* are also universal signs. Motioning toward yourself with your right hand means *come*, and a finger on the lips means *silence*. Most signs are made with the right hand. Amerinds who wanted to let you know they had heard something would cup their right ears with their right hands.

Other signs are more descriptive. To express the term *heavy*, both hands were stetched out with palms up, as if hefting a weight. A *bird* was represented by keeping the elbows close to the body but holding the hands out horizontally at shoulder level with palms down and imitating the beating of wings. To represent numbers from 1 to 10, as people do everywhere, Amerinds held up the equivalent number of fingers.

NUMBER SYSTEMS

Such simple numerical communication was insufficient for the Aztecs and Maya, who had a very advanced number system. They did not use a base 10 (decimal) system the way we do. Rather, they used a base 20 system. For example, they figured the number 862 as 232:

$$2 \times 20 \times 20 + 3 \times 20 + 2 = 862$$
$$(800) + \quad (60) + 2 = 862$$

In the decimal system, we figure it as:

$$8 \times 10 \times 10 + 6 \times 10 + 2 = 862$$
$$(800) + \quad (60) + 2 = 862$$

The Maya invented the zero long before it was introduced into Europe. This remarkable feat allowed them to make very complex computations. For example, they figured out on what day of the week December 31, 90,000,000 B.C., had occurred.

Zero was not introduced into Europe until Arab mathematicians brought it to Spain about eight hundred years ago. The Arabs probably got it from India. Before that, European scientific computations were limited; the Maya could use numbers far greater than the Europeans. Even the great mathematical achievements of the Greeks could go only so far without the use of zero.

Just as the Plains Indians used their fingers to indicate numbers, the Aztecs used hieroglyphs of fingers to record numbers from 1 to 20. (Sometimes they used dots or circles.) Twenty was represented by a flag, and 400 (20 × 20) by a feather. They would write 862 as:

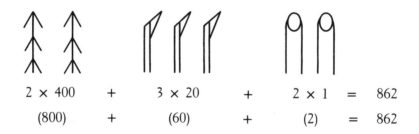

2 × 400	+	3 × 20	+	2 × 1	=	862
(800)	+	(60)	+	(2)	=	862

CALENDARS

Perhaps the most important use of the number system was for the making of calendars. We have already seen that Amerinds used their knowledge of astronomy to determine the succession of the seasons and the length of the year. The Mesoamericans recorded these observations on calendars. They devised several different calendars, probably for different purposes.

For religious purposes the Aztecs and Maya had a 260-day calendar. Each day had a name and a number; there were twenty names and thirteen numbers. This allowed for a combination of 260 since each day had a separate designation. You can understand how this works if you imagine two interlocking cogwheels or gears.

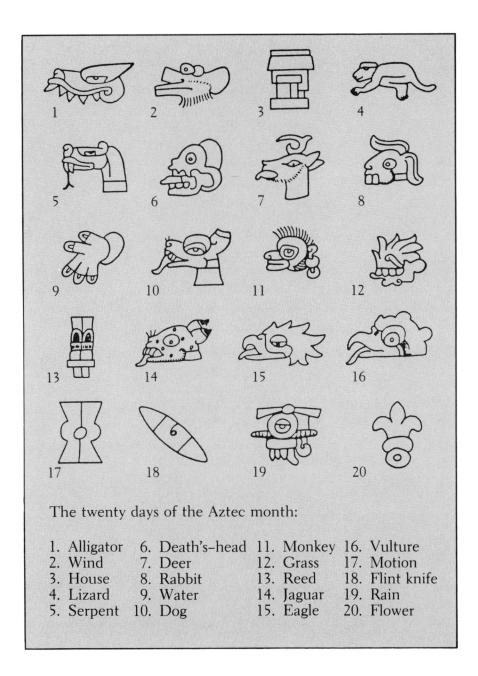

The twenty days of the Aztec month:

1. Alligator	6. Death's-head	11. Monkey	16. Vulture
2. Wind	7. Deer	12. Grass	17. Motion
3. House	8. Rabbit	13. Reed	18. Flint knife
4. Lizard	9. Water	14. Jaguar	19. Rain
5. Serpent	10. Dog	15. Eagle	20. Flower

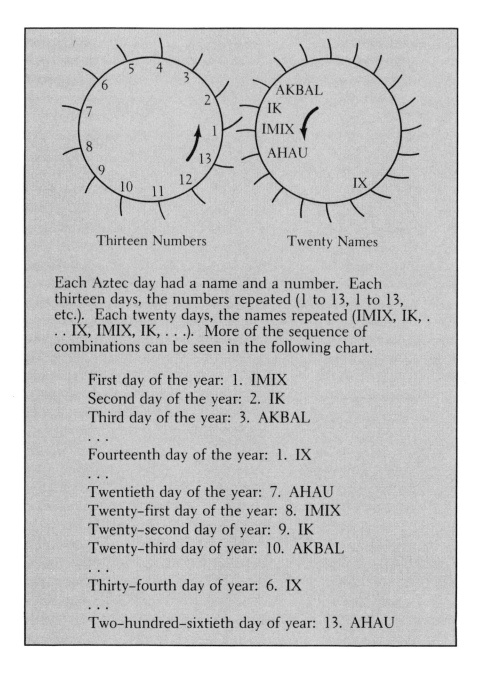

Thirteen Numbers   Twenty Names

Each Aztec day had a name and a number. Each thirteen days, the numbers repeated (1 to 13, 1 to 13, etc.). Each twenty days, the names repeated (IMIX, IK, . . . IX, IMIX, IK, . . .). More of the sequence of combinations can be seen in the following chart.

First day of the year: 1. IMIX
Second day of the year: 2. IK
Third day of the year: 3. AKBAL
. . .
Fourteenth day of the year: 1. IX
. . .
Twentieth day of the year: 7. AHAU
Twenty-first day of the year: 8. IMIX
Twenty-second day of year: 9. IK
Twenty-third day of year: 10. AKBAL
. . .
Thirty-fourth day of year: 6. IX
. . .
Two-hundred-sixtieth day of year: 13. AHAU

The first—the number wheel—has thirteen teeth; the second—the name wheel—has twenty teeth. Each day, each wheel turns one space. After thirteen days—at the end of the first cycle—all thirteen teeth on the number wheel have been used, but only thirteen of the twenty teeth on the name wheel. The second thirteen-day cycle again goes through the thirteen number-wheel teeth, but on the name wheel it uses teeth fourteen through twenty and then repeats teeth one through six. The third thirteen-day cycle uses teeth seven through nineteen on the name wheel. After twenty cycles, all 260 possible combinations have been used, and a new year begins.

The Maya and Aztecs also used a simple solar calendar for agricultural purposes. This calendar was composed of eighteen months of twenty days each for a total of 360 days. But they knew that there were approximately 365¼ days in a year, so they left five blank days, which were called "extra" or "useless" days and had no names. These five days were considered unlucky; people born on them were thought to be unfortunate. To make up for the quarter-day, they had a leap year similar to ours.

Another Mesoamerican calendar was used to record historical events. As we have already seen, there was a calendar to compare the "Earth year" with the "Venus year." There was also an accurate "real-time" calendar that measured the solar year—the time between one crossing of the zenith by the sun and the next crossing. This the Maya figured as precisely 365.242500 days, almost identical to the best modern measurement of 365.241298 days.

The North American Indians were less able at computing. However, the Hopi devised a Luni-Solar calendar that had thirteen lunar months. They adjusted this calendar so that it was never more than one day off for calculating their important solar festival.

Amerinds used mathematics in many ways besides making calendars. The Hopewell Mound Builders built an eight-sided struc-

ture 660 feet (200 m) long on each side at Newark, Ohio; they certainly had a knowledge of geometry, and they used surveying skills in their projects.

All Amerinds needed to count in their everyday life. They counted the number of deer they killed on a hunt; they counted the number of sheets of paper they had to send to the Emperor; they counted the number of rows of maize they planted. The Inca tied knots in pieces of string to help them keep track of the numbers they counted; the North American Indians drew pictures of the number of objects; and the Mesoamericans recorded them with hieroglyphs on paper.

TRADE AND TRANSPORTATION

The most important use for counting was in trade. Amerinds had no regular system of money; occasionally they used rare or beautiful items such as jade or special bird feathers as payment. The New England tribes liked wampum—beads made from white (and

The Stone of the Fifth Sun,
the Aztec Calendar Stone.
At the center is the sun god.
The four squares around his
face symbolize the four earlier
suns, or eras, of the world.
The next narrow band shows
the twenty Aztec day signs.
The outside ring is formed
by two fire serpents.

Eskimos with an umiyak in 1935

sometimes purple) shells they found at the seashore and along river banks. The Maya were fond of cacao beans, which were hard to come by, and often used them as a standard of exchange; for example, one hundred cacao beans could be exchanged for one slave.

Mostly Amerind trade involved barter: swapping so many deerskins for so much obsidian; so many seashells for so much cotton cloth; so much copper for so much honey. Trade was carried on throughout the Americas; goods were exchanged from South America to Mesoamerica and all over the North American continent. Amerinds traded salt, rubber, tobacco, vanilla, animal skins, dried fish and meat, turtle eggs, pearls, shell beads, mica, and flint.

Usually the Amerind traders carried their bundles on their backs. Pack animals were used only after the Spaniards introduced horses from Europe, except for the occasional use of llamas and alpacas in South America and dogs in Mesoamerica and North America.

The Plains Indians would hitch dogs to a travois—an open basket dragged on poles—to move heavy loads. The Eskimo used dogs, too, to pull sleds over the snow and ice. For sea voyages, the Eskimo had umiyaks, or large wooden vessels covered with skins and propelled by wide oars. In British Columbia the Indians used huge seagoing dugout canoes that they made from giant trees that grow along the coast. In Tierra del Fuego and in New England canoes were made of tree bark. And on Lake Titicaca, between Bolivia and Peru the Amerinds used balsas—large canoes made of reeds to carry people and cargos.

The most common means of transportation was walking. Amerinds walked great distances all over the Americas, carrying heavy loads, usually in baskets.

MAKING DO

Basketry was one of many crafts that Amerinds practiced. They also made beautiful pieces of pottery; they wove and dyed cloth; they developed tools for farming, hunting, and fishing; they made musical instruments; they invented games for their leisure time; and their rock art and jewelry are still admired today. But baskets were of major importance in the lives of Amerinds. They were used for many purposes: for carrying things, for storing things, and even for cooking.

Because the Anasazi made and used such a large variety of baskets, they are called the Basket Makers. They made large conical baskets that fit on their backs so that they could carry loads. They had huge globular baskets, some as big as 120 inches (3 m) in circumference, for storing food. They had shallow trays that they used for winnowing grains, or separating out the chaff by fanning, and for sun-drying seeds, fruits, and vegetables. They covered the sides of their baskets with clay and baked them in the sun until they were hard enough for carrying water and cooking. (Remember, they cooked by dropping hot stones into containers of water.)

North American Indian
basket patterns

Other Amerinds also had special baskets. The Paiute used basketry to fashion winter huts out of reeds or bark. They also made conical baskets that could be held on the hip when they collected seeds. They used a fan-shaped wooden beater on the heads of ripe grasses and then swept the seeds into the basket. The Plains Indians made large shallow baskets for their dog-drawn travois. Sometimes baskets were used for traps in hunting and fishing. We already have seen that on Lake Titicaca Indians made basketlike canoes out of reeds.

Basketry is the art of coiling and sewing, or weaving flexible materials into useful objects. The materials most used by Amerinds for basketry were vegetable fibers: reeds, rushes, sedges, grasses, and straws. Baskets were first made by coiling bundles of grasses or rushes. The layers were fastened together with sewing strips of the same material. Amerinds used an awl made from a pointed bone or stick to punch holes in the bundles so that the sewing strips could be threaded through them. To weave baskets, one strand is put under or over another. This can be done in a great many patterns; by using different-colored fibers, Amerinds wove beautiful designs into their baskets.

Basketmaking is a very old skill. Like fire, it was probably "invented" in many places at different times. Archaeologists have found baskets made of reed and leaf fibers by the Indians of Peru about five thousand years ago. But since vegetable fibers disintegrate over the years, it is likely that basketmaking is a much older craft even than that. Basketmaking came before pottery making; perhaps the skill of pottery making itself developed when clay was used to cover baskets.

POTTERY

Pottery, too, was "invented" at various times in various places in the Americas: by the Maya in Mesoamerica, by the Pueblo Indians in the Southwest, and by the Iroquois in eastern North America. Archaeologists are constantly finding older and older Amerind relics. Recently in Florida they dug up a pale orange clay pot that they believe to be about four thousand years old. They found it in some five hundred broken pieces; when they fitted the pieces together, the pot was 14 inches (35 cm) in diameter and 10 inches (26 cm) deep. The color had resulted from baking: the iron in the marsh clay that they used for pots turned pale orange when it was heated.

Clay pots are more fragile than baskets and so are not practical for nomads—people who wander from place to place. But once Amerinds settled in villages and became farmers, they began making pottery. At first their vessels were very crude—mere lumps of clay that were shaped by pressing in with the thumb and then by thinning the walls between the thumb and finger in a spiral movement. These first pots were dried and hardened in the sun.

Clay is formed by the decomposition of rock minerals, mainly feldspars. Feldspars are very common; they are the main components of gneiss and granite, the two rocks that make up three-fourths of the earth's surface. The decay of feldspar into clay is caused by the chemical action of carbon dioxide and water on rock surfaces when and where no air is present, as in marshes and bogs. The different colors of various clays are due to their mineral contents. In the Mississippi River Valley and in the Southeast the clay is red because of its iron. In the Southwest the clay is white or buff because of a substance in it called kaolin.

If natural clay is mixed with the appropriate amount of water, it becomes pliable and can be molded into a great variety of shapes. These shapes can be retained during drying and hardening processes. Among Amerinds air drying usually involved two steps. When about 15 percent of the water in the clay was still left— when the pot was somewhat hard but not brittle—the rough edges were scraped off with a wooden paddle. When only about 3 percent of the water remained, the pot was ready for firing, which Amerinds did in open fires. Clay loses its chemical ability to combine with water and becomes similar to a moderately hard stone at temperatures from 840°F (450°C) upward.

Since Amerinds did not use wheels, they could not throw pots. *Throwing* means spinning a lump of clay on a rapidly rotating wheel while guiding it and shaping it with the hands. Instead of throwing, they used the coiling method. Clay was rolled into "sausages" 1/2 inch (1 cm) to 2 inches (5 cm) thick that were built into the pot spirally. Each coil was pressed and smeared into the one below. Each circuit of the pot could be formed by a separate sausage of clay; the process could also be continuous. When one sausage of clay was used up, another was joined to its end.

The pots were made in many forms and shapes. There were small bowls and large bowls. There were ladles and dippers. There were elaborate pottery pipes for smoking tobacco. There were large storage jars. There were pots in the shape of gourds. There were "effigy" pots—pots in the shapes of people, gods, or animals.

If a pot being made was big, the Anasazi tied it loosely with cord to hold its shape as they molded it. These cords left marks on the clay that were then baked in, forming the corrugated designs common in Anasazi pottery. Other tribes used different designs. The Hohokam decorated their buff-color pots with red lines of crested quail or rows of dancers holding hands or figures carrying burden baskets. The Anasazi used black decorations on white bowls; others used white and black on red. These painted designs were made with earth colors that Amerinds found in the soil.

Pottery making
with coils

PAINTS

The most common earth colors were the various shades of red made from hematite, an iron oxide. The Paiute enriched these reds by heating ground-up hematite. The second most common color was black, made from manganese ore, charcoal, or roasted graphite. White was made from chalky deposits, from gypsum, or from kaolin. Amerinds got greens and blues from copper ores, and they got yellow from limonite, another oxide ore. These earthy ores were ground up fine in a metate and were often molded into cakes for storage for later use.

Paint that was applied to a piece of pottery before firing would harden on the pot and form a glaze. A color could be applied uniformly or in a design that became part of the pot and would never rub off. Paint could also be applied after firing. Designs could be painted on with brushes made from the frayed ends of yucca plants or from bound masses of fiber as those of anole. Other Amerinds used pointed sticks or their fingers.

Some archaeologists believe that pottery decorations developed from the art of body painting. Body painting is often wrongly called "war paint." Originally Amerinds painted their bodies to protect the skin from wind, sun, rain, snow, and insect bites. They used the same earth colors that they used for pottery. The designs indicated the rank of the wearer or had religious significance, such as protecting the wearer against evil spirits during warfare or sickness.

ROCK ART

For pictographs—rock paintings—Amerinds mixed pigments with animal oils, blood, egg whites, or vegetable oils. The Yokut used sap from milkweed, which they mixed with the crushed seeds of a wild pepper.

The most common form of Amerind rock art was not painted

at all; it was engraved on stone. Stone carvings—petroglyphs—can be found by the thousands all over the Americas. (Remember the stone records of the 1054 supernova.) Most petroglyphs were made by pecking—striking the surface of the rock with a sharp piece of harder stone—or for a more precise design by chiseling—using a hammer stone to pound on a pointed chisel stone. The design was usually started with a series of dots that were then joined into lines by continued pecking.

In soft sandstone a design could be carved with lines an inch (2.5 cm) or more deep. In another kind of petroglyph—gravel petroglyphs—small stones or boulders outlined huge figures in gravel. Some gravel petroglyphs, like those the Nazca made about two thousand years ago in southern Peru, are nearly 5 miles (8 km) long.

METAL AND SHELL ORNAMENTS

Except occasionally to start fires, Amerinds did not use iron until after the Europeans came. However, they knew how to use other minerals and metals for many purposes. The Maya, Aztecs, and Inca removed gold, silver, and copper from rocks by smelting. But most Amerinds simply beat the metal nuggets they found into the shapes they wanted. The Nazca made wooden sculptures of human heads that had copper mouths, eyes, and noses; they even added strips of copper to represent tears falling from the eyes. The Hopewell used hammered copper for tools such as knives, for armor breastplates to protect them in battle, and for ornaments such as beads, headbands, and earplugs.

Self-adornment was important to Amerinds. Archaeologists have found many pieces of beautiful and intricate Amerind jewelry. For example, the Pueblo Indians made necklaces from as many as six thousand tiny shell beads; each was pierced with a hardwood drill. They also made strings of small copper bells, and they used turquoise to make designs that they inlaid into shell ornaments.

Perhaps the most interesting jewelry technique was one the Hohokam invented for decorating the seashells they got by trade from the Gulf of Mexico. They used various designs: horned toads, snakes, birds, other animals, and many geometric patterns. These designs were not painted or scratched on the shells; they were slightly raised—they were etched!

First, a Hohokam drew a design on a shell with resin or pitch. Then the shell was steeped in an acid solution made from the fermented juice of the saguaro cactus fruit. The unprotected part of the shell was eaten away; when the pitch was scraped off, a raised design was left. The Hokokam had invented an etching process about 450 years before European armorers applied this process and more than 500 years before the German artist Albrecht Dürer used it in Nuremberg in 1515.

WEAVING

The Amerinds' most important body adornment was their clothing. Over the years the cloth fibers have disintegrated, like the ancient baskets. But from the fragments of cloth that remain we know that they were artistically woven. Archaeologists have found pieces of cloth in the Chicama Valley of Peru that are more than three thousand years old. They were woven with a combination of cotton and bast fibers for strength. Animal fibers—such as wool or silk—can also be woven into cloth, but Amerinds mainly used vegetable fibers.

The fibers were first cleaned and then spun. Spinning is the process of drawing out the fibers—pulling them lengthwise—and twisting them into long, continuous threads. At first fibers were spun by rolling them between the palms of both hands or between the hand and the thigh. The thread was then wound on a slender stick or spindle. Eventually the spindle became part of the spinning process. Amerinds drew the fibers between the hands and then rolled the spindle on the thigh to twist the thread. The twisting is the most important part. All fibers are not entirely smooth; they have microscopic rough edges that cause them to stick to each other when twisted. Twisting gives elasticity and strength to the spun threads.

The threads were woven into cloth by the "under-over" method also used in basket making. But since cotton threads are not as rigid as reeds and rushes, weavers needed a way to stretch the warp—the threads over and under which the weaving is done. So weavers invented the loom. Like fire making and pottery, looms were invented at different times and in various places. The simplest was a horizontal loom in which the warp was stretched between two beams fastened to four pegs driven into the ground.

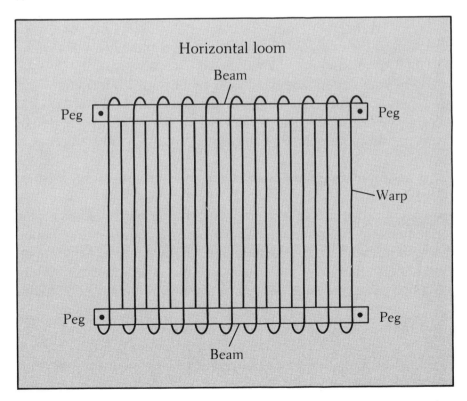

Amerinds devised a variation on this simple loom called a backstrap loom. Instead of being pegged to the ground, one end of the warp was attached to a post and the other to the weaver's belt. The weft—the horizontal threads—was then woven under and over the warp. Various designs were made by changing the number of warp threads that the weft passed over and under at one time.

Once woven, the cloth could be dyed or printed or both. The most important dye the Aztecs used was cochineal. (We have already seen that they used a hieroglyph of the cochineal insect and the cactus on which it lives for the name of the town Nocheztlán, where most of the dye was made.) Before the Spaniards conquered Mexico, Europeans did not have a good red dye; cochineal became second only to gold as an export product after the Spanish conquest. A fleet of three ships sailed for Spain but was shipwrecked off the coast of Louisiana. It carried about 660,000 pounds (300,000 kg) of cochineal powder—an expensive loss!

Amerinds understood the dyeing process well. They knew that the pigment had to be combined with a mordant. A mordant is a substance—usually an acid—that combines with an organic dye to form an insoluble colored compound, or lake, in the fibers of a fabric.

The Zapotecs of Nocheztlán and their neighbors the Mixtecs dried cochineal insects thoroughly, then ground their bodies into a powder in a metate. They used only the females because their body tissues contain the deep maroon pigment. Then they boiled the powder with crumbled tejute leaves, which contain an acid, and added acidic fruit juice such as lime, as the mordant. They obtained different shades of red by varying the amount of cochineal powder used and the kind and amount of acid added.

Amerinds used similar methods to make blue dyes from indigo bushes and purple dyes from murex snails. Tribes that did not have cochineal or indigo or murex, such as the Navajo, processed plant roots, bark, and earths to obtain the dyes they used on their cloths.

If Amerinds wanted a design on cloth, they used small stone or clay tablets about ½ inch (1 cm) thick with patterns engraved on them. The patterns were stylized birds, lizards, other animals, or geometric designs. An engraved tablet was dipped into a dye or paint and then stamped on the cloth.

FARMING

The cotton for the cloth was hand-grown. Amerinds used few agricultural tools for raising their crops. The Aztecs used stone axes to clear the ground; then they planted the seeds with a digging stick called a coa. They made a hole with the point of the coa, dropped the seeds in, then covered them with the side of the coa. The Iroquois used a hoe made from the shoulder blade of a deer to clear the ground. Then they, too, used a digging stick.

The Inca improved on the usual digging stick. They made the stick taller than a man and added a pedal near the bottom that was curved to fit the sole of a foot and a ram's-horn-shaped handle near the top. A farmer would hold the top of the staff in his left hand, then bear down with his right hand on the handle and with his right foot on the pedal, thus increasing the efficiency of the tool. The depth of the hole was controlled by the height of the pedal.

The seed-hole method, using digging sticks, was used for all crops: corn, beans, squash, and cotton. Only fertilizers and irrigation systems differed from place to place. On the New England coast Amerinds used fish heads for fertilizer; in Peru they used guano—bird droppings. Guano was distributed by the government, as it is today; the birds are still protected by law.

Mesoamerican Amerinds began watering their crops by hand about 7,000 years ago, and about 2,800 years ago they began irrigating their fields. In Peru they used the water of the rivers that drained the Andes. They built ditches to divert the river water and aqueducts to carry the water over the ravines. One such aqueduct was about a mile (1.6 km) long and 52 feet (16 m) high. Some of the Peruvian irrigation systems were as much as 75 miles (120 km) long. A few are still in use.

In the desert of Arizona the Hohokam also had long irrigation networks that diverted water from the Gila River to their fields. More than a thousand years ago hundreds of miles (kilometers) of canals crisscrossed the valley near Phoenix. Some canals were as much as 33 feet (10 m) wide and 7 feet (2 m) deep. This network was a remarkable achievement since the Hohokam used only wooden digging sticks and stone hoes and had to carry the dirt away in baskets.

Not all Amerind irrigation systems were so complex. The Paiute used temporary ditches. In the spring, when the snow began to melt, they built dams of boulders and brushwood across the beds of the mountain streams; they diverted the water over the hillsides to their fields. The Pueblo Indians also built ditches along the slopes to carry water to their terraced fields.

The most spectacular systems were the Mexican **chinampas** (literally, "floating gardens"). These were artificial islands 15 to 30 feet (5 to 9 m) wide that were created by digging canals to drain swamps. The Mesoamericans drove stakes into the soft bottoms of the swamps and connected them with woven twigs to form small enclosures. Then they scooped up the mud and dumped it in the enclosures until the "islands" rose a foot (30 cm) or more above water level. Several crops a year were grown on the well-watered, fertile chinampas; they also provided space for dwellings. The great city of Tenochtitlán was built mostly on chinampas. Food for its more than 250,000 inhabitants was brought in from other chinampas in canoes that traveled the canals.

WEAPONS

If pre-Columbian Amerinds had few farming instruments, they were equally lacking in hunting and fishing tools. But their ingenuity helped overcome both deficiencies.

At first hunters threw wooden spears at animals and hoped to fell them. Later they added stone tips to the spears. These tips are called points and were made of a hard stone such as flint. Thousands of points have been found; they vary greatly in size and shape.

Archaeologists believe that some of these points were used as much as twenty thousand years ago to hunt the prehistoric horses, giant ground sloths, and mastodons that then roamed the Americas. The points are named after the locations where they were found; for example, Folsom and Clovis are names of towns in New Mexico. Points have also been found in Arizona, California, Wyoming, Nebraska, Nevada, Utah, Texas, and many places in Mesoamerica and South America.

To increase the effectiveness of their spears Amerinds invented the **atlatl**, a grooved wooden device that made possible a harder cast of the spear and a straighter flight so that the spear tip hit its target with greater force. The atlatl and spear were also used for fishing by the Eskimo and other Pacific coast tribes from Alaska to Tierra del Fuego. The Eskimo added ivory tips made from walrus tusks to their harpoons. The atlatl was eventually replaced by the bow and arrow, which became the main weapon not only in hunting but also in warfare.

Amerinds' ingenuity showed itself in the ways they used these meager tools. The Paiute added poison from the glands of snakes or the spleens of wild goats to the tips of their arrows to make them more deadly. They also dammed up streams to make pools and then added poison from leaves, stunning the fish trapped in the

Stone-age projectile points attached to
spears or lances were used to kill and
possibly dress Ice Age mammals. The points
are named after the places they were first
found and reflect different styles. From left to
right: (top) Clovis, Alberta; (center) Agate
Basin, Dalton; (bottom) Clovis, Folsom.

pools so that they could be speared easily. The Kwakiutl built salmon traps—long wicker baskets into which salmon swam as they made their way upstream to their spawning grounds.

The Patagonians used **bolas** to fell fast-moving game. *Bola* is the Spanish word for "ball." Hunters attached two or more heavy round stones to the ends of a strong rope and hurled this bola so that it entangled the legs of an animal. In parts of South America Amerinds made blow guns out of hollow plant stalks and blew (shot) clay or stone pellets at birds and small game. The Nootka in the Pacific Northwest used heavy logs from the big trees that grew there to construct traps into which they drove deer.

MUSICAL INSTRUMENTS

Hunting and warfare were usually carried on with rituals; the spirits of the animals had to be appeased. The rituals involved not only body paint and special clothing but also much banging of drums and blowing of horns. Drums and horns were the principal musical instruments that Amerinds used. They made drums from hollow logs or from the shells of large tortoises, or they fashioned them from clay. The Ojibwa used short sections of hollowed basswood logs for the frames of their drums; the tight bottoms were also basswood. They poured a little water into the frame before they stretched a dampened buckskin over the top and attached it with a wooden hoop. The water inside gave the drum its special sound.

Other percussion instruments used by Amerinds were copper balls, rattles made from gourds or turtleshells or carved from wood, and bones, both animal and human, that were rubbed against each other or tapped to make a sound. Their wind instruments were trumpets, horns, and flutes made from conch shells, hollow lengths of wood, or baked clay. Amerinds had no string instruments.

77

Music was very much a part of pre-Columbian life. They sang and chanted and danced, accompanied by instruments, not only as part of their rituals but also for entertainment.

RUBBER

Amerinds were fond of games as well. One game, played with special balls, had an important effect on world technology. These balls were about 6 inches (15 cm) around. They were made of solid rubber. They were used throughout South America and Mesoamerica; two have been found as far north as Flagstaff, Arizona. The rubber came from latex, the milky juice of tropical trees and plants.

Amerinds knew the other properties of rubber besides its resilience, or ability to bounce. They used it for waterproofing cloth and for making containers and shoes.

The Spaniards, the first Europeans to see rubber, were not particularly impressed by the balls or the waterproofing. They were more interested in gold and cochineal. But when the French arrived they saw the possibilities of this "new" substance and started exporting it to Europe. There for a century or more it was used mainly for elastic bands and pencil erasers.

For a long time natural rubber could be obtained only in the Americas. But in 1876 some seeds were smuggled out of Brazil and planted in other tropical countries such as Sumatra and Malaya.

6

WE STILL DO IT
THE AMERIND WAY

Our use of rubber—both natural and artificial—is only one of the many things we still do the Amerind way. Some of the foods we eat, some of the medicines we use, and some of our modern designs are derived from Amerinds.

The Amerinds used only natural rubber, which comes from the para rubber, caucho, and manihot trees that grow only in tropical climates. But scientists have long tried to produce rubber profitably from other plants that grow elsewhere. One of the most successful sources is **guayule**, a shrub that grows wild in the Southwest and in northern Mexico. *Guayule* is the Aztec word for "gumball plant"; it is between 2 and 3 feet (60 and 90 cm) tall and is a member of the sunflower family. Pre-Columbian Amerinds used latex from guayule for rubber, but it has never been a reliable source since the quality of the latex varies from plant to plant.

Recently, a scientist at the University of California has successfully cloned guayule. When he finds a plant whose properties are desirable—for example, good latex yield and drought resistance—he clones it. The cloning process grows new plants from small pieces of living tissue. The cloned plants have all the desirable traits of the parent plant. They can be grown to produce seeds for commercial production in places other than the tropics. Our modern need for rubber far exceeds that of Amerinds. We need it for such varied items as truck tires and surgical gloves, for gaskets and hoses, for overshoes and balloons. So we keep trying to improve on the Amerind way of producing it.

Scientists are also experimenting with almost-forgotten Amerind food crops. They hope that these will provide us with higher-yield, more nutritious grains. Quinoa, the grain that grew so well high in the Andes, is becoming popular once more. It is frost- and drought-resistant and has a higher protein content than wheat. Research is also being carried out on amaranth, a broad-leaf plant used by the Aztecs. It too has seeds high in protein, and the leaves can be used as greens, like spinach. But there are also foods that we have used for hundreds of years and still prepare the Amerind way: corn tortillas, succotash, maple syrup, cactus jelly, and popcorn.

One Amerind product that we use differently is cocoa. The Maya and Aztecs prepared it as a drink called **chocolatl.** Cocoa was introduced into Europe before either tea or coffee; we still drink it today. But most cacao beans today end up in the form of chocolate. Before the American Revolution, a chocolate factory was set up in Boston and named for the founder's grandson, Walter Baker. Another famous chocolate maker was Pennsylvania Dutchman Milton Hershey. Americans consume chocolate in great quantities as hot chocolate and in cookies, pies, puddings, cakes, and candy bars. But Europeans—especially the Swiss, Austrians, Belgians, and Dutch—eat even more.

Centuries ago, the Mesoamericans chewed **chicle**, the latex of the sapodilla (sa po DEE a) tree. Sapodilla trees grow in the tropical rainforests. They can be tapped for latex only infrequently and only during the rainy season. Today, chewing gum is still made from chicle. The latex is boiled until it reaches the correct thickness (a process similar to making maple syrup) and then is molded

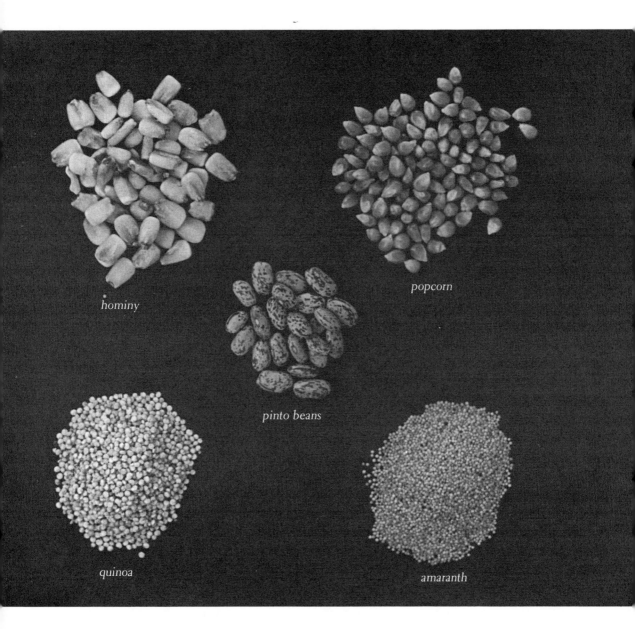

hominy

popcorn

pinto beans

quinoa

amaranth

Foods of Amerind origin

into blocks for use in producing chewing gum. Candy, popcorn, chewing gum—the gifts of the Amerinds!

Some of our simpler medical remedies are also based on Amerind practices. We use herb teas and bark teas as they did. A popular cure for poison ivy is still a poultice made from crushed stems and leaves of jewelweed. Amerinds smeared earth on wounds to heal them, a procedure that Europeans considered disgusting until the middle of the twentieth century, when penicillin was "discovered." They then learned the healing property of the mold contained in the earth. The medicine men used jimsonweed as a soothing drug; today we distill the chemicals in this flower for use as a tranquilizer.

We do not copy many rituals of the medicine men, but occasionaly a rain dance seems necessary. In 1970 Minnesota was experiencing a severe drought. The farmers, who were of Scandinavian ancestry, were upset after a cloud seeding failed. What to do next? Fifty of them resorted to the rain-dance ritual. They were "rewarded" by a thunderstorm that brought 2 inches (5 cm) of rain to their parched land.

While filming the Disney film *Nomads of the North* in Banff, Canada, in 1959, there was no snow—and at that time no snow-making machines. The delay was costing the producer thousands of dollars a day. Finally the producer called for a rain dance. In the cold Canadian climate, snow began to fall!

Our Amerind heritage includes many other practical arts: building with adobe brick, coloring cloth with cochineal dyes, using cochineal in foods and cosmetics instead of red dye number two (which has been found to cause cancer), inlaying jewelry with turquoise and other stones, weaving blankets, making sand paintings, and using Amerind designs in modern textiles and jewelry.

Some of these we often forget have an Amerind origin, but occasionally we are reminded. One advertisement for a mail-order house features brass belt buckles in "Haida-style Bear" and "Kwakiutl-style Raven" designs.

Traditional Amerind designs are used
in contemporary jewelry.

STILL TO COME

Part of our Amerind heritage is visiting archaeological sites, especially in the Southwest, Mesoamerica, and South America. At last count there are 1,830 such sites in Mexico alone. At least 2,000 more await exploration; we believe that many pre-Columbian sites have not yet been discovered. Like the legends of lost gold mines that are part of the folk history of many places, there are also stories of unseen and untouched Amerind habitations.

One of these is Lukachukai, a fabulous, legendary Anasazi city in northern Arizona. A Navajo told two traveling priests about it in 1909 and showed them a beautiful olla—a ceramic water jug—that was definitely a relic of the Anasazi. But no one has since found a trace of that Navajo or of Lukachukai. Perhaps one of our readers will be the fortunate discoverer.

Other sites like Gallina Towers, Machu Picchu, the Mississippi Mounds, and the Nazca Lines need more decoding. The Gallina Towers were untouched and unseen until 1933, when a hiker wandered into a secluded canyon in northern New Mexico. There, in an area 35 miles (56 km) by 50 miles (80 km), he found no less than five hundred towers dating from about the year 1200. The towers are 25 to 30 feet (8 to 9 m) high, with the walls made of sandstone blocks and joined with adobe mortar. At their bases, the walls are 6 feet (2 m) thick, and the tops have parapets for defense like European castles. There are no doors; entrance is by means of ladders to the roofs. Inside they are richly ornamented. The walls are smoothly plastered and covered with drawings of plants, birds, and flowers. The floors are paved with massive slabs of carefully fitted sandstone. And along the walls there are hollow benches or bins that contain such things as leather pouches, decorated seashells, brightly painted wooden prayer sticks, clothing made from deerskin, beautiful featherwork, dance masks, horns and bows and arrows with flint arrowheads.

*Ruins at Machu Picchu, the fabled city of
the Incas high in the Andes Mountains in Peru*

Although the site is close to the Pueblo Indians, the people of the Gallina Towers were not related. Who were these people? Where did they come from? What happened to them? There were sixteen bodies found in one tower. Had they been killed in battle? Were others driven off or taken as slaves? These are only some of the questions still to be answered about the Gallina Towers.

There is also much to be learned about Machu Picchu, the ruins of a fortress city high up in the Andes Mountains of Peru. We are not sure just what all the buildings were. Were they astronomical observatories? If so, with what heavenly bodies were they aligned? The date of its construction is still uncertain, as is the reason for its abandonment. But one thing we do know is that it was built by the Inca. The Peruvian government considered it a national insult when an American movie that starred Shirley MacLaine and that was filmed in Machu Picchu claimed that extraterrestrials had built it. The government ordered the filming stopped, and the script had to be rewritten.

It was not atypical for the filmmakers to attribute Machu Picchu to extraterrestrials. For some time now the Nazca Lines on the desert along the southern coast of Peru have been called Messages to the Gods, Ceremonial Walkways, and Runways for Interstellar Space. The lines are from 3 to 5 miles (5 to 8 km) long and take the form of plants, animals, and abstract patterns. They are hard to see from the ground; some are visible only from an airplane. They were made about two thousand years ago when Amerinds outlined the figures with darker surface rocks, leaving the lighter sandy desert soil exposed. Because of lack of rainfall in that area, oxidation is very slow, and the rocks and sand have hardly changed color since the time they were first laid out.

What was the purpose of these lines? They probably were not astronomical pointers; you cannot sight easily on that desert.

Nazca lines in Peru

There is still much to find out about these huge birds, spiders, flowers and geometric patterns on the desert floor.

Similarly, we have still to determine the significance of the shapes and forms of the Mississippi Mounds. And we have to find out why there are twenty-eight spokes in the Big Horn Medicine Wheel. Why were so many Mesoamerican cities built with the same orientation? Even though great progress has been made, there is still a lot of decoding of Mayan hieroglyphs left to do.

Perhaps the most tantalizing mystery is the possibility of pre-Columbian association with Europe. Archaeologists believe that except for the Norse explorations along the northeastern coast of the Americas in the eleventh century, Amerinds had no direct contact with the rest of the world until the Spaniards came. But if that is so, how is it possible to account for a carving of a definitely Negro head made by the Mixtecs about a thousand years ago, or a Mayan head made in about A.D. 300 that resembles a Mediterranean merchant prince from Phoenicia, Greece, or Syria? And how did Roman and Jewish coins from the second century get into the Cherokee ruins in Kentucky and Tennessee?

Most curious of all, where did Amerinds get the idea of making toy wheeled, animal-drawn carts that have been found in Mesoamerican digs? We *know* the pre-Columbian Amerinds never used wheels!

GLOSSARY

adobe—a sun-dried brick made from clay mixed with straw

archaeoastronomer—a scientist who studies the astronomy of ancient peoples by analyzing the remains of their cultures

atlatl—a spear thrower

bola—a rope-and-stone combination used to kill game

cacao [ka KAY oh]—the tree that bears the seeds—cacao beans—from which cocoa is made

cairn—a pile of stones at the center of a Medicine Wheel

chicle [CHIK el]—sap chewed by Amerinds, used today in chewing gum

chinampa—an artificial island made by digging canals and draining a swamp; a "floating garden"

chocolatl—a cocoa drink of the Maya and Aztecs

coa—a digging stick

cochineal [koch a NEEL]—a bright red dye made from the cochineal insect

codex—a book made from strips of deerskin or pressed tree bark, sewn together in long panels and folded like a screen

equinox—one of the two days of the year when the sun crosses the plane of the earth's equator, making night and day of equal length all over the earth

guayule [yoo ah YOO lay]—a shrub that yields latex

hieroglyph—a pictorial symbol representing an object or word

heliacal rising—the rising of a planet or star on the eastern horizon just before sunrise

kiva [KEE vah]—a meeting room

maguey [mah GAY ee]—a plant used to make paper

maize—the grain we call corn

mano—a hand-held grinding stone

metate [may TAH tay]—a slightly hollowed slab used with a mano for grinding

petroglyph—a carving on stone

pictograph—a painting on any of various materials: animal skins, rocks, tree bark, shells

pueblo—a communal dwelling; also, Amerinds who lived in a pueblo

solstice—one of the two days a year when the sun is at its greatest distance from the celestial equator

FOR FURTHER READING

Baity, Elizabeth Chesley. *Americans Before Columbus*. New York: Viking, 1961.

Baldwin, Gordon C. *How Indians Really Lived*. New York: Putnam, 1967.

Beck, Barbara L. *The Aztecs*. New York: Watts, 1983.

Colby, C.B. *Cliff Dwellings: Ancient Ruins from America's Past*. New York: Coward McCann, 1965.

Fichter, George S. *American Indian Music and Musical Instruments*. New York: McKay, 1978.

Fronval, George, and Daniel DuBois. *Indian Signs and Signals*. New York: Sterling, 1978.

Glubok, Shirley. *The Art of the Southeastern Indians*. New York: Macmillan, 1978.

Glubok, Shirley. *The Art of the Woodland Indians*. New York: Macmillan, 1976.

Grimm, Wiliam Carey. *Indian Harvest*. New York: McGraw-Hill, 1973.

Meyer, Carolyn, and Charles Gallencamp. *The Mystery of the Ancient Maya*. New York; Atheneum, 1985.

Morrison, Velma Ford. *Going on a Dig.* New York: Dodd, Mead, 1981.

Scheele, William E. *The Earliest Americans.* New York: World, 1963.

Scheele, William E. *The Mound Builders.* New York: World, 1960.

Tunis, Edwin. *Indians.* New York: World, 1959.

Von Hagen, Victor W. *The Sun Kingdom of the Aztecs.* New York: World, 1958.

Yue, Charlotte and David. *The Pueblo.* Boston: Houghton Mifflin, 1986.

INDEX